Thievery

AKRON SERIES IN POETRY

AKRON SERIES IN POETRY
Mary Biddinger, Editor

Seth Abramson, *Thievery*
Steve Kistulentz, *Little Black Daydream*
Jason Bredle, *Carnival*
Emily Rosko, *Prop Rockery*
Alison Pelegrin, *Hurricane Party*
Matthew Guenette, *American Busboy*
Joshua Harmon, *Le Spleen de Poughkeepsie*
David Dodd Lee, *Orphan, Indiana*
Sarah Perrier, *Nothing Fatal*
Oliver de la Paz, *Requiem for the Orchard*
Rachel Dilworth, *The Wild Rose Asylum*
John Minczeski, *A Letter to Serafin*
John Gallaher, *Map of the Folded World*
Heather Derr-Smith, *The Bride Minaret*
William Greenway, *Everywhere at Once*
Brian Brodeur, *Other Latitudes*
Jeff Gundy, *Spoken among the Trees*
Alison Pelegrin, *Big Muddy River of Stars*
Roger Mitchell, *Half/Mask*
Ashley Capps, *Mistaking the Sea for Green Fields*
Beckian Fritz Goldberg, *The Book of Accident*
Clare Rossini, *Lingo*
Vern Rutsala, *How We Spent Our Time*
Kurt Brown, Meg Kearney, Donna Reis, Estha Weiner, eds.,
    Blues for Bill: A Tribute to William Matthews
Sharmila Voorakkara, *Fire Wheel*
Dennis Hinrichsen, *Cage of Water*
Lynn Powell, *The Zones of Paradise*

Titles published since 2003.
For a complete listing of titles published in the
series, go to www.uakron.edu/uapress/poetry

Thievery

Seth Abramson

The University of Akron Press
Akron, Ohio

17   16   15   14   13   5   4   3   2   1

ISBN: 978-1-937378-66-0 (CLOTH)
ISBN: 978-1-937378-67-7 (PAPER)

This book has been cataloged by the Library of Congress.

The paper used in this publication meets the minimum requirements of
ANSI NISO Z39.48–1992 (Permanence of Paper). ∞

Cover: *ghosts #6* by Chris Friel, www.chrisfriel.co.uk. Used with permission.

Thievery was designed and typeset in Stone Print by Amy Freels and printed
on sixty-pound natural and bound by BookMasters of Ashland, Ohio.

for my parents

CONTENTS

I

SLOWDOWN

What you cannot face
you face—that's your direction. In houses in cars
      in cars that become houses
the event stage is dark
then revealed, the longest story chapter by chapter,
what makes someone somewhere
despise you. How will I know when it happens?
      It'll be a long drive,
you'll know.
Across the street is a street fight
in which a man without shoes shrieks to no one
particularly

but not to me. The alarm clock is pushed away
from the bed and a man is lifted up to a white van.
      His arm falls to signal everyone back
to the races. Or it's midnight,
      and men and women are in each other
in buildings,
      and some have never gone anywhere
but there, over and over. What apartment are you in
      they will be particularly asked
and they will say
the same as before, Mother. What state are you in?
Again. The question has their scent and the answer
their form. It is the fight of their
lives, if they walk away from it. And then that's that,
or nearly.

GUNBROKE

South is adventure, north cold but also shelter,
and in the west
an end. It is south then north then west, the trail.
East is finished. To tell it right
it must be half in green
ignorance and half beneath the groan of a wheel
still turning and stained by smoke. The tone of it
is that everyone's been turned out from somewhere
by someone,
and afterward crossed a place they ran wire across
and a place they built a rotwood storm-closet,
and pounding atop where a mass grave was made
too small and then on to a place
nothing startles the horses.
You can put a pistol to one and leave it shrugging
in a stand of alfalfa
and not one other moves near or away. And then
south of course
are long plains of plain men and plain women all
hatless and gunbroke. Blood livens them
to themselves, their own hard lips, their own cold
singing. They build a city to hold it, and somehow
that lasts.

SOME DROWNED ARCHER

Where the waterway gives out there is mud
and when the mud gives out
people. On display for heaven their things
arrayed in the dark. A horse fallen into
the track made for it.
A longbow can be had for fourteen dollars
at the flea market in Carlisle
but it won't fire. And a bear that won't eat
at the state fair. Love without blossom
everywhere. Some man has fallen in the mud
and the history of that
is clear. Raised up to one arm fell again.
Raised his head to see how things would be
dropped it back.
The sun dries a thing out for something else
to use. And the use of a thing
is never used. Or the history of it exhausted.
An archer shoots. That's what an archer does.

THE COUNTRY WEST

Follow a target that big
you don't ever reach it, you end up lit
in the nightlands and bagged
in a single.
No sun but the black hole in your horse.
People go west for things,
sometimes entirely. I myself will move
from spring to fall
for you, or right to left—dawn to dusk.
The ass you are to the ass you could be.
The country west is puttering

in the mouths of birds, and the mouths
of birds
are opening and closing slowly up there
to see you parched down below
with your white hat all covered in flies.
And the freedom of wild horses to die
as horribly as they do

is the best thing about standing quietly
with this light
behind you. What's a vulture
but a man who arrives early
and unready. A ferocity that quits on you.

Follow a target that bright and that big,
you never wonder what time it would be
if you could run backward.
        I mean the small strummed cord
in the slit in your back.
The shape of the thing that crushes you.

ALL YOU PLOUGHBOYS

What I found at the back of the wood
made my hairs fray,
and what I saw over the weeds in the water
were stars, some of which were sweet to me
many years

though I knew they were just
lamplight from the homes of people like me

capable of anything. At the back of the wood
I am capable of anything.
The blanket of black water is being shaken
by a relentless mother
on the far shore,
the lake of weeds is being tussled
by the breath of its father.
The actual stars can no longer be seen because
the light from town

pollutes.
But then they say nowhere light is
is unnecessary.
Leave the light on for me
I say to the people who love me
when I am sure
to do something horrible. I am by the lake
at one
wearing leaves from the back of the wood,

        I am sure
to do something horrible. Half the wood is
halfway there.
And half this town is half in love with itself,
        but me I go all the way.

THE WOODS IN CONCORD

       Down by the oaks tonight
you might still find a musket, boys,
but stay lively
for the feral cats in the underbrush.
In the forest we carved from a still
greater forest
there was the lesser forest
we lived in.
Have you seen the boys of means
up at the old stone brook,
they will say
you feel pretty narrow
for a good boy. They will ask you
if you fall every night,
and for what. You'll hear the story
of three decades of winter
and worse luck for someone else's
daddy. They will sell what they got
for free
and give up freely what no one else
would buy.

       Down at that tumbledown
a boy might find himself
a black charger with wet haunches—
no, it's a tree. But mark it,
the boys of means
say, whinnying and playing at older
in a fortress up the canopy,

if we'd wanted to whittle you into
a gun, we could have,
if we'd wanted to light you up, we
could have,
if we'd wanted to strangle you
in a crib of twigs and moss
here in the grim dark
behind your house, we could have.

NAUGHTY BOYS WELL
AND TRULY PUNISHED

At the bottom of a trunk full of limbs
he keeps a photograph of Adam
        and *her*
in which the two stand jowl to jowl
and are naked
        but confused. Nothing fits.
There is a second photo in an inset
in the first
in which he and she are bleeding
in an interesting way. There's a limb
in the locked trunk
that attaches to similar effect. I am
at the beginning of things
and my blood
is well and truly concealed, he thinks.
He would snap the limbs in the trunk
one by one
        but it's not time
yet. Every boy's blood is every boy's,
so I cannot hide long,
he thinks. But I also cannot bear her
seeing me. That makes it hard.
And so he turns away another night
and every boy on the block turns away
and Adam in his colorless garden
        turns away
and every Friday up and down streets

and streets off streets
boys bend their small willing bodies
in interesting ways
when she comes to the door and says
      it's happening.

HOMETOWN COURAGE

The minute hand was bent.
At eight
it was almost eight. At nine
almost nine.
I have almost been made
many times,
        once in Concord

with two girls from Stow.
One held me down
while the other one
went to it on top of a guy
with a large, clean pickup
out back. He looked over
from the other side
of the four-poster. This is
good, he whispered.
Yes, I whispered back, this
is good.

•

The minute hand was longer than
usual. Beneath it
a man was standing over a girl,

his arm reaching above her
his fingers
curled around the minute hand
like a truncheon. Each minute
there was a click
and the hand pulled him closer.
Can I get you
anything, he said. Can I get you
anything.

•

The sofa was too short for anyone
to lie down on. People were sitting

who wanted to be lying
on one another, people were lying
on the floor
who should've been sitting upright
in cabs. Only three girls passed by
that way,

and only one would sit. Only one
is ready, a man with a pickup said
to me. She's not from around here,
he said. That means—

I know what it means, I said. I can
see it.

A COSTUME FOR CROSSING
THE RAINBOW BRIDGE

                                        If there is a door open
anywhere in the house,
I cannot fuck. If there is a television on
and there is a cage on wheels
on the television,
I can fuck even if all the doors in the house
are open. But they must all
be open. I have not been a good man for long
and this makes me scream
pleasingly
under the right conditions. It is impossible,
impossible,
she says, and asks what I have to say about that,
though I don't know
what is impossible so I don't know
what I have.
I know there is mischief underground—
the door down to the basement is unlatched
and a crown of wind
has pushed it slightly ajar; like so, I say. Don't
touch me, she says.
And why don't I go down into the darkness
of the landing, and then the foyer,
and then the greater hallway,
and then the lesser hallway, to close this door
that goes down into the dank?
Is there not a woman upstairs and a fresh set
of pillowcases?

Yes. But there is also a black clump of rags
down there
behind the steadiness of the washing machine,
and in the black, but only on nights like these,
a body forms

                         and its nose is cruel—
it smells me perfectly. Its fingers will rip me up.
No, no, there can be no fucking anywhere, now.

THINGS UNSO

If the wind takes the house
it will be someone else's
soon enough, and they too
will find it cold. What breaks
breaks open. After a house
one finds oneself in a wood,
and after too long in a wood
one finds oneself sullen
in heaven. Someone else lies
in my bed now so I can't
sleep any better than they do.
To be lost is to be connected
interminably.
When they turn in my bed
the whole house turns, and I
turn, and the wind is emptied
through my own and theirs
and through a common door
to some place I do not know.
If things fall far enough apart,
they are all equally gone.

THE PUSH

He went down into the unified image
        of a town
at midnight, not one town made of men
with specific desires and a general lack,
but one board stood up
beside another and another to set apart
        a general desire.
Every object there at the valley base
in the sharp of its vector
sang the one word they had made for it.
There an object
could only be as the man who is praying
is in a church
        wherever he is.
There every word was worth its mouth,
and went from mouth to hand
so men could handle words as currencies
and default.
Unnatural work was no work at all,
there.
        He went down because up
was beneath him
and the event stage was dark as a clock.
And the people there slept well
in their indoors
because everything but the commons
was behind them.
He went down into the unified image
of a town

where the commons was dark enough
for the dark
to hit home—
         for an antagonist to emerge
and make his play.

II

PARACOSMICS

They come from the woods three by three
and I pass the time a world or two
watching.
The great brown foxes' bulb-dark noses bob
as they pass by on two legs
in black masks,
burlap sacks over their shoulders. Inside
the children. I smell in the deep of a sack
an unfortunate boy but for the eyelashes
who's dreaming he's in his mother's womb
as she's raped
        by her work in the laundries.
Is this enough for you
he calls
and I see he means me. You just keep on,
boy, three by three as before.
With a clever little knife another one makes
a hole
        and his eyes starpoke
from the black. Stars are just endless knots
says his fox
and sews his sack up. But we were speaking
of heaven and hard-ons,
that's clear. An unfortunate boy but for all
those lashes, and yes I suppose
that does it for me. I forget to get a name
but I do shake the hand
        of every passing burglar
but one. Him I roll because he's took a girl

and we don't. We won't. She worms pinkly
onto the grass beside the track
and asks me to stay with her and she means
always. She's asleep before I can answer her
                with the one word
that makes this end and be like it never was.

PUBESCENCE

Sometimes he thinks of the girl and sees
stars in the shower.

In the stalls of the market
women write girls and men write boys.

Poison is something given.

Sometimes a particular girl makes him
think of himself.

Sometimes he looks down and looks up.

Men on white horses can't remember it
any better than he does.

First, the little man opens his door.
Then he cannot catch what skitters away.

Wrath is autumnal and fathered.

Sometimes an always lingers. Meanwhile,
churches.

Because I cannot go, because I will not,
because I haven't yet been asked.

A pearl of inestimable price. But not his.

THE BETTER KIDS

They cloudbank
in the windows, single-armedly brought up
from tiny hearts of meat
to tiny raised fists, out of snowed-up ways
where wolves in fantasies of histories
are nursing boys,
and where boys are pounding uphill
with a killing speed. Up into themselves
they launch themselves, up into monasteries
black behind the capes
of nightwatchmen, into the many cymbals
of orgies
of women and men, half-women half-men
behind a seventh-story façade
the boys will soon be joining them behind.
Growing lakes
beneath their feet. Growing agonies
into men, and the hunting parties men join
like circled cinder blocks. Some men,
like hunters' foaming palfreys, are the men
who don't survive it.
And the girls are even worse at it than this—
the sad sex of sad boys.

FIRST RESPONDER

The light arrived the light died
among idle boys waiting on their wind
of which I was one. All around boys arrived
        and went, boys were returned
one by one to heaven's cold shoulder.
Excuse me, I'm speaking, I had to say to one,
I am a box of words. Thursday boxes arrived
and opened and then I was in a box traveling
        to where a boy finishes himself.
Like all the foundering ships firing their guns
all at once
to call for aid. But there are so many ships
        and so many guns,
it's a sea full of stars to anyone on shore.
So we are dangerous
to no one else. Now it is Tuesday noontime
and I mean for everyone. So when I say
you see what I mean,

I mean that. If you lie here, it's your wheel
and tiller, you stand by it
or fall into the blue trough. That's sailing.
        The blue comes, it sees you,
and then the blue is everywhere else and only
everywhere else. There's a woman.
        Only one thing tastes good
at a time, and the dark looks right indefinitely.

Then the corpses of thieves are doing business
        in the dark on a dock

and it is at a distance the play before the play.
Soon everyone has
        someone else's life beneath their feet,
and is moving with metronomic grace between
two open doors,
        and then lamplight accrues in a corner
where something as spotty as its memories
is awake and waiting
        with a ball-peen hammer. After that,

it's bloody bones for everyone. You say
it won't be so
and that's unso. We must do this thing again
and again
        with someone else's body in the dark
and it hurts them.
Despair for us is a giant character that keeps
resolve in a hip pocket. I was with you
        in a place we ought not to have gone

and it seemed we would both say love when
the light came back again—
        to a place it ought not to have come—
and you reached for your side, and I for mine.

LOVE SONG
FOR ANOTHER BOY

       The war took me into a room
and raised me. It took me hard,

       it could not live without me
it said,
       but it did, it lived a long while
without me
       in a room by a knife

       and a woman and a lake,
of course a woman because that's how
I am.
       A woman took me into a room
and held me, she did her war
cry and showed me
       how on the far side of her
there would be the finest war

there had ever been. And it was. It was
the finest,
       it killed many men.

THE MARCHERS

When we came to the crossing she said
how would you describe that flag
and pointed to the foothills and I said
I would say
        on fire. We rode the long way
past the lines of men
and the places they were coming from
and the places they were going to
and the places some were resting awhile
and some were resting
a longer while. When we came out
at the top of the valley
the flag was so far below it looked just
she said
like brushfire. And see how it catches
the trees around it I said
and some of the men also she added
and I nodded
and we made camp by seven and hobbled
the horses. That night there were screams
in the valley
and some were happy. Some don't know
what's coming she said
or I imagine
I was still asleep in my roll like the others.
I slept a long while.
        And the flag under her saddle
sat warm and flat all night
and held its tiny breath until the sun rose.

GOOD FORM

When we lit our fires at night it wasn't much to see
people running. Someone said
quartermasters are the only middle men in the war,
and soon after a dozen or more escaped
through a black patch in the wood. In battle we say
       we will fight you
alone in the gutters, but also up to our thighbones
in war mannequins
we will fight you. Sometimes it's forgettable,
someone must remind us the seconds are running hot
in the deeper mines.
When we hear the dithering zargon of defenders
over the water, it gets the welterweights
gripping their nippled grenades. Some wave their hats
and are overawed. We forget positions. Someone said
everyone reaches the same sea,

but if galley slaves gather to watch through oarlocks
what other benchmen
have had the courage to do, do they cheer for them,
and is it slavishly? We can survive against either wall
of the stockade
       and still lose our middles to the diet.

       When we were there, we leapt from our holes
into bigger ones, we were pushed back,
we did it again,
we were only imagining we could walk through fields
filled with your fine faces. The sound of your sighing

      hanging indiscernibly,
splitting old flames into new shapes. And like always,
the minor ones
would die, and we'd sit in the deep grass and watch it
all night.

TRISOMIC DIALOGUE

                    Here she said
these are love poems about me.
He killed himself, you know.
No I didn't. Still she said I think
they're lovely.
I was in hospital, they told me.
They told me
I had a picture of us in Le Havre.
I was lovely. We
were lovely. He
was lovely. These are lovely also

let go of my hands please. I wish
I could. Let me see that one.
I mean
the poem. This one took a year
to reach me,
he was stacked six deep by then.
I remember that. How could
you. I know how these things end.
Here she said

this is a threat. Yes, it's a threat.
I don't know
how a person could die that way.
You mean sending threats
to the woman you love. I mean
a combination
of asphyxiation and electrocution,
that's the point

of that one. I thought the point
is he's dead. No the point is
we were in love. No the point is
a year's a long time.
No the point is that no one
who's been kissed can ever forget.

THIEVERY

                              At first I think
I don't love my neighbor's car, he can keep it
though yes I want it

because want is not love and cars are not
named hearts. What kind of waking is possible
on Monday, what kind of work is possible
on Tuesday. The new road says I love you
and step on my face
              I will not resist. But in a minute
it keeps its secrets, it holds you off like love
in its last year. You were born to love
in seizures, says spring, but you were born
to be just, says the woman. You were born
to wake,

says Wednesday, but will it still say the same
on Thursday. All I know is
I step over the border and say to him, I need
your car. He resists, we kiss unpleasantly,
we have arms not hands, it lasts all summer,
we fall into closeness
without contact, I mean to say his jaw breaks
wide open. I need your car, brother. I need
that goddamned car. I want to pull my face

out of the world, I want to crawl nakedly past
a hurtful opening, I want to be betrayed
              for the better,

I want to ride in a box that holds its lightning
like your car,
brother. I want to be struck and deserve it,
I want to ride down the street where the boys
show their guns to anyone,
and then later in a wood I want to watch trees
pointing guns
        at anything that moves.

ONLY

If locatable it is found, and if found is
lived in. If lived in
is died in, and as it caves in takes all in
and moves on. If it moves
        I see it coming, sometimes I do
I swear. I have been in the places things
were coming true
        that were unwanted, in places
things went
unwell, where things went and went

considerably far. Sometimes survivors
do not survive,
sometimes a home is remade anywhere
        anyone finds themselves
mistaken. I have seen that happening,
when sometimes nothing else
was happening,
        when on a Jersey barrier
a black car rested
no longer on fire, and mourners passed
with their engines no longer so loud,

and people waited quietly no longer so
ready to die.
And in their still heels and small spaces
briefly were not afraid
        of being somewhere else.

BRONX FLYWEIGHT SPARS

He made a portico in the dark with hands
and feet. If he moved toward the mirrors
he was larger, if he moved away
   the light shone on the fact of him
in a way he would soon forget.
Was he crying?
   There was a stance he knew

for that, so he made an antique fountain
   in the light
with his chin and his wayward beliefs.
Were they flagging?
Somehow it seemed the man up ahead
   and the man behind
   were moving together
against him, his size an approximation
of theirs. The coaches explained being
outnumbered
   another way,

   loneliness.
   He thought on that long enough
he was certain
there'd been tears. He thought about how
his nose had looked before,
how he remembered remembering that.
Which was precisely how he'd been taught
to see it.

THE FIRE DOOR

       Then he'd become very old
and he realized,
no,
it was only the standard suffering
he had. He was not a dark horse.
The fire in the barn would burn itself out
in time
       the way corruptible lights do

and yes, the fire would take the barn
and seventeen horses he'd always known
and his sister
       whose hard-won love he had
and a baby who'd come from
somewhere
       to become someone. All

       would be destroyed,
and destruction would once again be
the last lover
       of old things.
There was nothing he could lose now
he could not replace with the absence
of his better self,
and he still had his hard-won knowledge
of the fact
       he'd become

       very old,

and that it's best to keep an open fire
in a place
it can't touch or tempt. For him, a place
       he dreamt of
with more and more cunning each night.

III

CHRONOPHRENIA

I.

Could it make it better if he were a ragman
on the Mississippi, if the people on shore
were as dark in their furnace-lit rookeries
as crows in theirs, so he never came ashore
to spit at them
and trade. Could it be better
in the late autumn of nineteen twenty-seven
than now, could salted meat in a pack
taste more like the Mississippi
when belligerent lives were lived there fully
and you knew there had been a dispute
more than three miles across the water
because you heard it
the moment a man collapsed into the button
of his canoe.
The things a ragman hears after dark
he moves on from or loses
everything. Could it end badly here—
yes, right then. Spine mishandled by a man
with weathered wrists and God knows
what history. Could it make it better
to know your father, to never have bedded
with a sister
gone now. Could you hear someone's cry
on the Mississippi
over the dark, could you feel something
touching your nose,

making you squint into the black shores
left and right,
is that something somebody needs to do,
or should he be as quiet as a crow lining
its nest. Could he do it, if he had to do it.
Could anyone. If the thing had been oiled
and kept in a warm, dry place for so long.

II.

Level and fire, level and fire, but always
level first
when you're speaking to that one
they said. They called me out just two days in
on a lighter to New Orleans,
but I never dealt from the bottom
like they said,
only I once showed my piece
to a lady. They didn't like it much.
The bell end was wet
like a newborn left soaking
in a new-sawn forest
by a granddad stuck in the bottle. So one man
produced a knife
and then the other
and then the other. I had a grey claw
from a crow fallen
on deck by the first mate's.
You win, they said, now go.
Everyone is always in a way with the voodoo,
said Captain,
throwing my stowage
into the waves.
All right, so he weren't no captain,
but my father
I'd always followed that way.
He was going downriver
with me or no he said. That's how I lost him,
or as good as that. Or maybe
he never spoke to me
but over the commercials,
and only about the things he needed to know.

III.

At least someone has treated you
like a bear
and found out where you sleep
and come to that place
to lie
on your broad back. At least
there was a weight you could carry
for a time, there was a long cave
with few roots
and a trickle of water in the back.
At least someone is trying
to get there with a pickax and six
days' rations, with a headlamp
and eyes that will see for a time
congenially.
At least there was one Sunday
they lit a candle down in the valley
in the window of a home
you couldn't enter
but at least it's there. Could that be
something to remember
through December and past. At least
there are dreams
in which the right kind of bear
is living the right kind of life
for a bear,
and the right kind of dream is finding
you at last
while you starve gently in your sleep
like always.

IV.

Then there's a bump in the night,
then there's a bump in the day,
then there's a crash, I am needed,
what can I do. What
can I do. Then a fighter jet growls
in the heavens, a loudspeaker pits
into a rumble across the water,
then there is water and more water
behind that. A woman—well. Then
there is a depth to things, I am in it,
then I am out
of all things, then it is said of me
I am missing. But then. Then
there's a bump in the night,
then there's a bump in the day,
I tumble off an inimitable storm
and roll and roll downhill
down a hallway until my back blacks
on the handle of a door. And then
keys, then furniture, then utilities,
then a Persian, then some space
and some words and some silences
to regret. Then a crimson papasan.
A jetliner heads west, then another,
then another, then another,
then another, then another. I have
the capacity for west. North, south.
East I can't go, when I am there
I am closer to it and I remember
a woman—well. Then no, then yes,

then I need someone to be here,
then someone needs me to be there.
Then go. Then come. Then please.

V.

It was hardest when I held it,
and if it burned my palm I imagined it
but I imagined it well. It's hardest
to see it in the flecks of morning
between the trees, I know it's perfect
then, the way I do scrub pines
when it's just their shape over me,
just promise, and the rain sloughed
through the fingers of leaves
hasn't run down my face, or nests
spilled out anything
speaking with more silver than I do.
A man holds just one of these and
just once,

I have met the man who broke his
under his heel
at a brothel, and he crept out mad
from the furnace of his life. Blood
increases hue, and when your face
is struck
or a man leaps forward with a will
onto your back, the tone of it is up
and stays that way. It's the heaviest,
its touch is the tomb-weight,
the skin-binding, the form of desire
not without object
but for an object sitting centimeters
from the heart, that will kill the heart
if it moves, when you understand

that it may move.
And then it moves. And everything
after that, remains.

VI.

One day I have gone from the bed
to the door and thereabouts
I am confronted. I want to be told
where the hell
I am going. And though the words
are ugly
and the hands on the handle are
much too white
I accept them
for dinner. I dine out thirty years
in the space of a country
doorjamb. One day I go without
an address for forwarding
and I am in a doorway
speaking with the confidence of a

country doctor. There's a diagnosis—
the boy has not been seen
around his father
thirty years now, and the father
has not seen the man
of himself and so the boy neither.
Where the hell is anything
in this village,
where are the warm muzzles
and the bowels tricked to the rafters
as reminder? I mean to say that
soon I must accept
what I have to say for myself.
One day I've gone

wearing the mud of a distance,
I've taken on a name that's far
from a beginning. Still I find
that far is far enough, and for what.

VII.

At the end of traveling
I wear the road. Within my skin it is bad.
It's worse without—
the particulates of being nowhere entirely.
It spans from the West to a winterlit East
on a single lane with drops to the death
over both shoulders.
I walk on years, I touch with all the worst
minutes. I mean it takes its single traveler
to an outhouse on a black prairie, I mean
there's one chicken left, one purblind pig,
and they can't be killed
or not by me. On Sunday the doctor comes

and says not to worry, he will only open
along the edges. He finds them quick. He
has an uncertain nose, he learns in blood,
he reaches through blood and he's satiated.
What I say to him slinks down his smock.
So the road is the crown
of your head, you are sent inside by sunlight

he says. That burns it too, you saying that,
Doctor. But it's true, at the end of traveling
I am the largest
silhouette, everything behind me I colon
into a list of what I'm made of. Up ahead
the doctor waits again in his red armchair.
I hold the light above him as he reads me.
I have left more behind

than is ahead, I'm close to it now. Not so,
he says, it's the shoulder you hang from—
halfway to the end of both East and West.

VIII.

Does my being here make it there,
does news travel
in bad weather. Does a sporting life
bring an animal down, does it dress
competition in comfortable clothes.
Does clothing fit. Does the fitting
make the fit fine,
does the rain cord on the window
like a noose or the black rope
that brings electricity
to a dark, dry place. Taos is a place
one goes, Searchlight is
and Trocadéro, and Bloomington,
the consciousness of being celled
and Dubuque Street,
and Olbrich Botanical Gardens,
and an apartment that is yesterday
in which a man is hurting
an already hurt
woman. Does my being here, does
here being celled, make it there,
to a place someone hurt has gone
tripping to. Does the hunting end
with disorder in the brush
or silence on a pale mantle in Taos
or Trocadéro. Do you pay
for each silence, and if so
why start. Can I admit this thing,
can I clothe myself
in something like it, is it time now.
Does the time come. Does it ever.

IV

NO ONE IS KEEPING YOU HERE

                    A fool sees the same lake
a wise man does, and seeing it wants the wise man
to throw him in—

which a wise man will do, for the man who desires
          but doesn't act
doesn't breed, and the world doesn't need
more fools. A fool sees the same star
a wise man does, it falls with a clear trace for both,
          but the fool wants the wise man to catch it,
because wholesome food is for the wise,

and wholesome food is anything caught
in a net or trap. I saw by the lake a man on a bench
rapping out the words I love you I love you
with his fists,
          and I knew he was a fool
because he was sitting alone and outside the light
          the park lamps made,
and there are enough lamps for almost everyone
in that park, by that lake,
as there are almost enough lamps everywhere
lovers meet. I saw a man on a bench
and I saw he had been cut, and like all cut fools
he was forgiving,
he forgave,
          because a dead body forgives its injuries.
Dip every fool in the water

who likes being held by the ankles, who would see
        the faces of those he loves
inverted, who would see them frowning
and still believe that fortune smiles on foolishness.

DUST BOWL

There is always a man at the base of the gully
       facing the rain,
and children behind a doorjamb with ideas
of telling someone,
       and bright red preserves
       stolen from a neighbor's trailer
to reward them if they do,
       and a mother who's no fool
because times are harder than anyone's been
told. Inside, no waking life
lets no one know it won't happen for them,
not ever,
though the jam is sweet, and it has been all
       these years,
and the man looked sweet with hands down
at his sides
       and legs up on a hummock,
and everything that happens while the radio
is playing
is just like this. Now no one they ever knew
was singing a song
they would have liked to live, stuck in a box
but as sweet
       as all the years ahead would never be.

FIRST SERMON

They were spoken to from the hilltop outside the city
and the subject was children.
For a moment they were the many points of a crystal
whose origin
was ninety-one feet to the north and up a slight grade.
So each of them knew they were sharp
            and looks could kill. They were told that
difficult children were coming their way
and in numbers, and too soon, and also ungratefully.
They will not understand how their emergence drives
from the otherwise
you, said the voice, gently attuned. Mothers recalled
how once they'd been asked for their bodies
twice the same night. Fathers handled dropped cocks
and rolled their shoulders forward
like trolley carts. At the foot of a hill awash in the sea
we could say they were all in a church
but it would be like saying they'd been received
at a feast the color of description
in a city we did not know existed. Now look and see
how they pray
            on these children, drawing back their heads
to make certain the young can hear
the voice that is right above them and the green voice
they are speaking in to one another
and the voice above the hill that is eloquent and angry
and not for them
            to reason with or obey.

RED SHIRTS AND NO BOOTS

        Boys are marching unwatched
from elm to birch
wishing to be seen. Now and then
they pound their dirty chests
where inside it is spring and trees
stand up martially. I
they think
I. Somewhere seventeen goldenhearts

are rushing an embankment
on the thirty-seventh page of a novel.
And knights in some summer play
are waiting
to display the superior effectiveness
of heavy cavalry. I see them milling
at the corner of a stage,

positioning themselves
at the edge of always. We are caught
in this way
in the terrible beauty
of the suicide. Or a stone on a tomb.
Or a boy in his bedroom.

HY-VEE

The eyes of cashiers are hard to see out of, because
earnest lies are the hardest to get out of,
and how many teams have I worn
the uniform of,
and why when we beat the others was it beating off
I was dreaming of—

and what secret was I ever the holder of,
so when the team spoke of me softly behind a door
it was really me they were speaking of,
and not the afterimage of
what I'd always hoped to be a good example of,
a kind of cousin of
those young men my mother and some books
had told me of,
who could stand against whatever grief their gods
had dreamt of,
because something else had made the stuff
they were made of,
and there would always be a quiet life back home
they were still worthy of,
if ever they decided they had had enough of
the hard young men they'd always worn the colors of.

THE DOCK LIGHTS AT
CATTLEPURSE IN THE FALL

When the sun rose on a difficult thing
I made myself more difficult than that
and in this way became the center of attention.
I did what no sunlight had risen upon
        in any previous year—
I was pleasingly intolerant with gentle women,
I was gratefully urbane with friends. I adored

a local bureaucrat. According to the mob,
motivation is an infectious disease: Pretty soon
girls will be putting girls into bondage
without the necessity of a dinner date, and boys
will wax cars philosophically—

not because they've been beaten by their fathers,
but because they're asking for it. At some point
or another
        we all can. The sun omits us awhile
while outside
confessions are ingested in lesser coffeehouses.
When the sun sets on difficulty, there will be

an unappeasable moon with clouds on its hips
stumbling drunkenly over uptown churchlights.
A fatherly-looking figure
with shoulders in the rain. I am always a body

for atoms like this,
          a professional believer on those nights
someone I can't remember has left a Montauk
askew on my slipway
          because I also own one and also enjoy
its many comforts. Then the sun-up somehow
I've come to love again

comes again, and once again I'm certain a boat
still in the corner of the matter

isn't sinking,
          it's just being consumed by
present circumstances. And that I can live with,
or else.

SOUTH

The streets make in themselves more empty space,
and the people who live on them
are less welcome
in their own words. Those who are about to fight
shutter shops and slap their arms
        until under their arms their veins bark blue.
Those who are about to make love
reconsider,
and those who are merely about disperse
into their hidden lots. A red car full of guns begins
its daily shuttle.
        When the world was dark
all dangers were terminal, and no one could survive
who was only surviving. When the world was starlit
        beauty was careless
and went where it went and who with, who with.
The danger was heartbreak. Now everything insults
and the terminal science
is sleep, as those who won't fight to hold their own
believe it does more
        than anything else they fear could do.

WRECKER

Down below past the fire escapes
they are widening the street
and men are hurrying from men
and women are hurrying

to women. There are many streets
and some of them
are clean.
I have thrown from a high place
a child
and he has landed in a low crouch
and set off like a man

down the length of a street which
is untouched.
So I call myself an event
which I am.
I see myself in the up of cups
and in dangers that
never fall. Sometimes I am at a sill

looking through a fire escape into
I imagine
the holes of old outhouses,
though bedroom windows of men
living sheets to sheets and women
waylaid by capers
are the only actual slights
on the empty street. And sometimes
the air of the city lifts into the room

like a new translation of someone,
and there's a piece of glass
sitting at the base of a space heater,
and I find myself

speaking of myself in the past tense,
and I worry.

EKPHRASIS

The first Samaritan to reach the girl
in shambles on the pavement
and alive to the fact
she was not going to make it told her
she would. It was something
said to a girl who knew she would die
by someone
who agreed with that assessment.
But sometimes
it is important to represent a situation
not with angles of the leg or a context
but an awareness
       make no mistake about it
in thrall to
its timing. In the beginning, it is said,
everything is possible,
but in fact at the very beginning
nothing is. The representation is also
the end. Eventually there will be
functions—
       functions between people and
functions of.
Some deletions on street corners are
less recoverable than others. But Art
is not the catastrophe. In the dark
manifold of the city,
it takes first responders seven minutes
to arrive. When they do, the Samaritan
will be the first to say the girl is dead,
and that she has been dead
       for seven minutes exactly.

TRANSIT

          Everyone in the air is going
to Milwaukee; women are taking their silver off
in lines; someone escapes the terminal
with a guitar; friends do not cry for their friends
and husbands do not cry
for their wives; the voice above everyone's head
is reasonable,
the voice above everyone's head is familiar;
by now some of the men outside have lost their
hats, and all of the men outside
will need their hats; one bird then another banks

into a cloud-pier, while everyone in the air sleeps
and imagines a single searchlight
shining on them only, watching them walk about
and slam doors or masturbate, but also save lives
that cannot know yet
they are worth it. Ninety-nine doubtful climbers
silverless and sleeping know
                  not one of them knows
how far is far enough for any one man or woman
to travel.

A GOD FOR OCTOBER

The curse is speaking like in books
not in books,
        in treating bones as homes
not in homes
but on the road.
You are being chosen to die
as you speak,
        and what is worse you are
for speaking
the last choice of everyone.
Nineteen miles out from something
that makes the shape
of a tornado, you're the last choice
to see it that way. But when you do
see it—

        its gray face, its gray beard
wrapped around it,
and the one eye like an tractor wheel
crushing your hand—

when you see it
suddenly there's the tread right there
on your palm—
because it may actually be the wheel
of a tractor,
and well off the road, and October,
and your hand, and just about time
something you won't ever lie about
starts to happen.

HELLO THE HOUSE

He kneels by the creek to drink
his reflection and his catch-rope
trails him
the fourteen hundred miles to Jersey.
His arms cold rifles spent
      at his side, burying themselves
in the black moss of the bank
he drinks at. The creek
whatever its pitch
is still carrying him off like a message
who gets it who sends it.
The bank holds its own size and shape
readily
but not his. His sits in a Jersey walk-up
      with money at the fly
for everything but milk. And in corners
reckonless shadows
      and shadows of other kinds
and outside where a Jersey pine starves
a woman on a stoop holds a rope.
Back at the creek
his halter shrugs tighter under his chin
and the man he sees in the water
is dumbstruck. Probably she is in love,
he thinks. And probably downriver
there is another man bent by the water
who waits for love also
      and also cannot see what he is.

SAMSON AT THE PILLAR

At first he belongs to heaven the way
the water can by the ruined fencepost

the rainwater from the dissipating
cloud
                    needling the earth

the territories men are thrown into
like holes.

Then she has his head tenderly
between her knees, and he knows then
what leaves by the garden gate,
what wakes in the wild with great teeth
and too few.

At first love can be first, the same way
the unseparated trembling black earth
heaven holds close
                    is first,

the unseparated trembling white lambs
in their first blood, held,

the fire separating from a man's mind
heaven lets go—

at first, the portentous terrible temple
gonging the inebriates to new orgasms,

the simple stone
the tombs of the times are made from,

the six slaves surrounding their master
and over seven long days undoing him
and anything else
                    that heaven can do.

POEM FOR BATTERED MAN

On the morning the sun is loved
by a woman
       on the right side
of the bed, a platoon of red birds
detaches from a willow
       across the river
because they aren't in love with it
and it doesn't love them back.
       For the flying
flight is easy. I have to make rent
for her
and for myself. Soon there will be
a breakup
       way up the flagpole,
the flag will flutter down to cover
its country. Not yet. Now there is
a man or woman
       dying for a stranger
on every screen, in every country.
It's what we keep
watching for, why I stay like this,
why being just one day
       in this particular sunlight
is worth the cost I'm speaking of.

ACKNOWLEDGMENTS

Some of the poems in this book originally appeared, often in slightly different forms, in *Bat City Review, Cerise Press, Fairy Tale Review, Linebreak, Minnesota Review, The Offending Adam, Propeller, The Rumpus, The Southern Review, Washington Square,* and *Yalobusha Review*. My sincere thanks to the editors of these journals for finding time and space for these poems.

Special thanks to the editors of *Linebreak*, who published "A Costume for Crossing the Rainbow Bridge" in their 2010 anthology, *Linebreak: The Two Weeks Anthology*; to artist Elizabeth King, who, under the auspices of Western Michigan University, produced a limited-edition broadside of "No One Is Keeping You Here" in November 2011; to the Academy of American Poets, which selected "The Woods in Concord" as its Poem of the Day for December 23, 2011; and to Deborah Ager and Matthew E. Silverman, who selected "Hy-Vee" and "Poem for Battered Man" for the anthology *The New Promised Land: 120 Contemporary Jewish American Poets* (Continuum Books, 2013).

It would be impossible to list here all of the individuals whose love, encouragement, and support were critical to the writing of this collection. But among the many people deserving of special recognition and thanks are: Claudia Abramson, Robert Abramson, Amy Quan Barry, Oliver Bendorf, Mary Biddinger, Sean Bishop, Paul Borchardt, Danielle Burhop, Andrew Burtless, Kai Carlson-Wee, Brittany Cavallaro, Mark Cayanan, Sarah Crossland, Jesse Damiani, Louisa Diodato, Eden Dunckel, Matthew Dunckel, Lewis Freedman, Amy Freels, Josh Freeman, Zac Fulton, Mary Gannon, Wade Geary, Peter Gizzi, Matthew Guenette, Rebecca Hazelton, Matthew Herman, Sterling Holywhitemountain, Amaud Jamaul Johnson, Josh Kalscheur, Ken Keegan, Lynn Keller, Jesse Lee Kercheval, Ron Kuka, Kevin Larimer, Julie Larson-Guenette, Jane Lewty, Vicente López, Maurice Manning, Sam McPhee, Shane McRae, Judy Mitchell, Rusty Morrison, Hannah Oberman-Breindel, Jacques Rancourt, Nancy Reddy, Emily Ruskovich, Yuko Sakata, Valerie Stull, Cole Swensen, Ron Wallace, G. C. Waldrep, Dara Wier, Dean Young, Kevin Zifcak, Sarah Zifcak, and Stephen Zrike.

ABOUT THE AUTHOR

A graduate of Dartmouth College, Harvard Law School, and the Iowa Writers' Workshop, Seth Abramson is the author of two previous collections of poetry, *Northerners* (Western Michigan University Press, 2011), winner of the 2010 Green Rose Prize from New Issues Poetry & Prose, and *The Suburban Ecstasies* (Ghost Road Press, 2009). Presently a doctoral candidate (ABD) in English Literature at University of Wisconsin-Madison, Series Co-Editor for *Best American Experimental Writing* (forthcoming from Omnidawn in 2014), and a contemporary poetry reviewer for *The Huffington Post*, he has published work in numerous magazines and anthologies, including *Best New Poets* (University of Virginia Press, 2008), *Poetry of the Law* (University of Iowa Press, 2010), *AGNI*, *American Poetry Review*, *Boston Review*, *Colorado Review*, *Harvard Review*, *jubilat*, and *New American Writing*. In 2008, he was awarded the J. Howard and Barbara M. J. Wood Prize by *Poetry*.